KENNETH TURNER

FRESH FLOWERS

KENNETH TURNER

FRESH FLOWERS

TEXT BY SALLY GRIFFITHS

PHOTOGRAPHS BY ANDREW TWORT

ST. MARTIN'S PRESS
NEW YORK, NEW YORK

CONTENTS

INTRODUCTION
More than just flowers

Set your imagination to work when creating fresh arrangements and think beyond the usual range of flowers and foliage. Mix flowers with fruits and vegetables; experiment with deliberately clashing colours; and be inventive with containers for truly stunning displays with more than a touch of ingenuity.

ROSES
Le mot juste

Roses must surely be the world's most popular flower, whether the full-blown, old-fashioned species grown in country gardens or the neatly elegant, long-stemmed varieties available all year round from your favourite florist. Here they are displayed to perfection in these vibrantly coloured and sweetly scented spheres.

RIGHT
*Candlesticks
made from
terracotta pots are
enhanced with a
confection of small
yellow, pink and
red roses.*

CANDLES

RIGHT
*Candlesticks
made from
terracotta pots are
enhanced with a
confection of small
yellow, pink and
red roses.*

These arrangements never fail to surprise and amaze - "It's all so simple, so dramatic!" one friend declared. Such an arrangement in the centre of a table had "a rare dominance" another affirmed! And if a nearby table or sideboard is clearly yearning to join in the fun, a further duo or trio of these candle-holder arrangements will add enormously to the decorative scene. I indulge with both "climbing" and "quiescent" roses, using each in a way that reflects its natural preference.

10

A lush and romantic grouping of fiery red and orange roses, offset to perfection with cool rosemary.

Above
The rosebuds open gently during the warmth of the day, revealing their soft, velvet petals.

True loves

To my eyes, each of these works of art - portrait and pot-vivant - is a visual joy. I have always inclined to fulsome containers for flowers, and I have loved that remotely romantic Victorian lady for many years. How serenely she stands amongst those rich, rich roses with their vivid yet always elusive reds and rusts, cerises and corals. My choice for foliage is invariably rosemary. The combination is sheer perfection. Little wonder I always relish saying "roses and rosemary". To my ears, these are sounds made for each other.

LEFT
*A marriage of
stone and
terracotta, each
offering a perfect
partnership with
floral beauties -
as these two
settings show.*

RIGHT
*Sculptured heads
have, to my eyes,
a rare and
poignant
ambience,
especially when
linked with a
multi-coloured
garland of
summer roses.*

15

Floral exotica

The setting is simple – the results a floral fantasy. Which exotic background has influenced me – Jamaica? Africa? India? But, I remind myself, I'm still in my garden room in London. Everything evolved here from rather more humble beginnings. All I did was paint two terracotta pots bright yellow and add "spheres" of perfect yellow rosebuds plus a candle. And to continue the tropical theme, add a customized container made by enclosing a plastic bowl with rows of bananas, add a circlet of orange-toned roses and pile high with lemons. Quite a jungly composition.

17

GARDEN FLOWERS
Spring & summer glory

*Spring and summer are the most glorious times
of year for ardent arrangers, with gardens meet-
ing the constant demands for yet more flowers and
foliage. When you have such an array to play with, you
can afford to choose simple containers and let
the flowers speak for themselves.*

LEFT
An essay in the ever-popular blue and white: parrot tulips, white lilium tulips, white double tulips, and viburnum, all complemented to perfection by lovely lime green foliage.

Salute to summer

Here we are with our blue and white china again. Everybody's favourite. Perfect for the spring collection and a salutation to the oncoming summer with cornflowers, grape hyacinths, scillas, forget-me-nots plus euphorbia doing duty as the final touch. Altogether a pretty, decorative contrast of man-made blue and white ceramics and nature's profusion in blue and green. What was so especially rare about this splendid assembly was its low-toned grandeur. Not a vivid red, pink or violent yellow in sight, yet so soothingly beautiful.

RIGHT
Never allow containers to overpower your flowers, however rare. Flowers are too short-lived. Let them have their glory day.

LEFT
The simplicity of amaryllis in a terracotta pot works to perfection with an attractive bamboo support.

RIGHT
The cool shades of white and green set off to perfection: a marble bust, miniature metal candle-holders and terracotta pots with lilac and box leaf trees.

LILACS & LILIES

One of a pair of covetable eighteenth-century bronze candlesticks was set into a bowl covered with glued-on moss. A piece of scrunched-up mesh wire netting was moulded around the base of the candelabra and securely tied with reel wire. This made the candelabra a superb sponsor for the gorgeous red double tulips, arum lilies, wonderful lilac and super purple fritillaria plus a touch of veronica - very botanical - consorted into one solo exhibition atop its Indian table.

LEFT
Such a simple combination of candelabra and flowers is perfect for entertaining, allowing guests to see one another across the table.

ABOVE
The same effect on a smaller scale: a miniature copper bucket crowded with a gorgeous yet simple arrangement.

27

LEFT
*More powerful
and striking than
any other flower,
vibrantly coloured
anemones
dominate the
scene straightway,
becoming the
belles of the ball,
as you see here.*

BELOW
*A brilliant colour
setting given even
greater glory by
contrast: simple
container, grouped
candles and the
almost artificial-
looking gerbera in
breath-taking
colours.*

29

EDIBLE DELIGHTS
Fruit, vegetables & herbs

*Flowers are not the only thing to put in a vase
so don't limit yourself. Gather in a bounty of
vegetables straight from the garden (or the supermarket
shelves!) and create your own harvest festival. Artichokes,
mushrooms, peppers, rosemary, apples – the list goes on
and on. Relish the range of colours, shapes and
textures, and allow your imagination to run riot.*

LEFT
*Towering candle-
holders of herbs
such as rosemary,
bay leaves or thyme
- ideal for summer
evening tables.*

Extravaganzas

New variants for candle-lit tables. Why not have carrot-bound bases for your candles or a crowning sphere of Brussels sprouts? Quite a surprise for your guests. Or you could set your candles within columns composed of bay or eucalyptus leaves. Practical, decorative, surprising.

RIGHT
*The humble
Brussels sprout,
transformed as
decoration,
providing a base
for candles and a
dome atop the
carrot-wrapped
plant pots.*

APPLES

Evolving new ideas for centrepieces is always an entertaining pastime, usually a challenge and frequently a surprise. Here is a recent experiment of mine. A casual assembly of apples, roses and lilies serves as an unusually decorative centrepiece for a luncheon or dinner party, but glossy red apples would have looked divine with those glorious colours. Here I used green Granny Smiths.

LEFT
A mound of bright green apples in a wicker basket surrounded by a collar of roses and lilies.

ABOVE
Small willow candle basket filled with an arrangement of roses, dianthus, lilies, phlox and apples, providing the perfect decoration for a summer dinner party.

RIGHT
*A fun job:
camellias atop a
sphere of luscious
strawberries
resemble thick
double cream.
The perfect surprise
for a spectacular
summer tea party.*

RIGHT
*All the elements
in this stunning
piece are equal:
every flower is a
star, every fruit
is a star.*

ABOVE
*Fruit and flowers
also appear on
equal terms in
this spectacular
tour de force.*

My friends called this "an exercise in sheer sensationalism". They are probably right, but I wanted to see just how far I could push the borders of floral design. I halved the melons, scooped them clear and used them as containers filled with strawberries. I also think the bananas are at their best in crowds, hence these bunches performing a superb balancing act on the rim of an Italian terracotta vase.

LEFT
I do love colour, but I have a thing about white flowers. Hence these, set against dark green.

This is, without doubt, one of my most romantic floral settings. perfect for a party, wedding or an unashamedly romantic dinner. The silver container is the starting point, perfectly suited to the occasion. Then the flowers - anemones, ranunculi, lady's mantle, daisies and euphorbia. Plus a wayward touch - artichokes. I adore them.

Arranging a bowl of flowers in the morning can give a sense of quiet in a crowded day - like writing a poem or saying a prayer

Anne Morrow Lindbergh   41

BASKETS
The classic container

The wicker basket can be lifted from its humble origins to become an integral part of any arrangement. Here it provides the perfect receptacle for sprays of delicate orchids, gently tied to bamboo poles with lengths of garden string, set off by a mass of grey Spanish moss at their bases.

BASIC GREEN

This is, without doubt, one of my most favoured groupings in one of my most favoured spots: an interplay of greens set in a splendid Victorian basket on my wrought-iron horseshoe garden seat. A trio of treasures! Little wonder, then, that I seem so eager to show this gorgeous selection of lime greens, including euphorbias, viburnum, stately stems of dill and dramatic foliage.

RIGHT
I have a passion for lime greens, probably because I love the spring which, for me, is essentially these magic colours.

Green is the fresh emblem of well-founded hopes. In blue the spirit can wander, but in green it can rest.

Mary Webb

Here tulips bloom as they are told

Rupert Brooke

Explosions

I love to create these mixtures of tulips or hyacinths and using them like explosions of paint coming off a palette, just bursting out in great strokes - a veritable blast of colour. You can combine the hues anyway you like: a warm mix of reds, pinks and oranges, or a cool classic springtime blending of blue, yellow, pink and white. And once again, of course, more gorgeous old baskets.

BELOW
A long-lasting and sweetly scented arrangement of lilies set in one of my favourite Victorian baskets.

RIGHT
A Turkish basket with mixed lilies, crown imperials, foxgloves and those marvellous green arum lilies, plus enchanting Solomon's seal.

ENCORE

GRAND FINALE
As simple as this…

*What better way to conclude this book than
with a celebration of grand, imposing,
triumphant and truly flamboyant arrangements. There
is always an occasion where nothing short of the biggest
and the best will do. Or, make any day a special one by
creating a grandiose bouquet. Here, a superb decoration
includes apple and cherry blossom, glorious
lilac and tendrils of trailing ivy.*

50

LEFT
*A perfect interplay
of colours - both
in flowers and
objets d'art.*

BELOW
*Close-up of the
gently dominant
major theme:
white lilies.*

This floral arrangment draws all the decorative elements of the room together. The colour scheme focuses on green and white, using arum lilies clustered in the middle, surrounded by euphorbia, viburnum, lilac and dill in an unusual black Warwick vase, set on a black marble side table. This makes for a classic, romantic drawing-room decoration, injecting brightness to what would otherwise be a quite ordinary corner.

Remember that the most beautiful things
in the world are the most useless; peacocks
and lilies for instance

John Ruskin   55

RIGHT
The quintessential arrangement emphasizing the glorious colours of summer. Note how the objects work in harmony with the overall ensemble.

Now this is what I call a summer decoration: a traditional drawing-room setting with a very large, classic urn. The main floral feature is the gorgeous golden choisya which has the loveliest blossoms at this time of the year. Then there are those wonderful snap dragons; dramatic splashes of orange dahlias, peonies, pink stargazer lilies and gorgeous pale mauvey-blue delphiniums, and masses of ivy cascading onto the table below.

EXOTIC

An eighteenth-century Buddha contemplates a variegated floral setting of ginger plants, monstera leaves and palm leaves. The unusual arrangement of stark architectural leaves and flowers is perfect in tall, cylindrical glass vases. This is a refreshing departure from traditional decorations, and one which is both exciting and restful at the same time. The marvellous Indian batik that I found in the Victoria & Albert Museum is the perfect background.

RIGHT
Display architectural arrangements in simple, plain glass cylinders for an eye-catching effect.

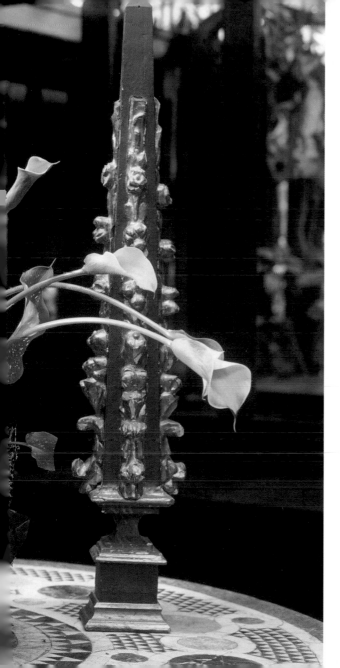

LEFT
*Decorating with
the brilliant help
of an old square
plastic bucket
covered in moss
and preserved
magnolia leaves.
Long-stemmed
lilies bow
elegantly from
on high.*

61

LEFT AND
ABOVE
*These two
photographs
illustrate how
a dominant
arrangement can
work equally well
against the*
*traditional setting
of an elegant
drawing room or
in modern
wooden urns on
an eighteenth-
century console
table in a small
hallway.*

ISBN 0-312-183143

Design by Lisa Tai

All photographs by Andrew Twort except:
Page 10: Kiloran Howard
Page 24 and Page 63: Marie-Louise Avery

Printed in Italy

First published in Great Britain by Weidenfeld & Nicolson

First St. Martin's Edition: May 1988

10 9 8 7 6 5 4 3 2 1

ACKNOWLEDGEMENTS

The author and publishers would like to thank the following for providing items for photography:

Nicole Fabre Antique Textiles
592 Kings Road
London SW6
Tel: 0171 384 3112

Guinevere Antiques
578 Kings Road
London SW6
Tel: 0171 736 2917

Myriad Antiques
13 Portland Road
London W11
Tel: 0171 727 7154

O.F. Wilson
Queen's Elm Parade
Old Church Street
London SW3
Tel: 0171 352 9554

William Yeoward
336 Kings Road
London SW3
Tel: 0171 351 5454

Many thanks also to the Kenneth Turner team: Simon, Barry, Laura, Karl and Christopher.